REAL ESTATE BRAIN (FOR SALE):

7 HACKS TO HELP YOU BUY LIKE AN EXPERT

JP FLUELLEN

This book is dedicated to my wife, Sheri, who has put up with me over the years; my four children, who endured countless nights without daddy; my sister-in-law Sonja, who pushed me to dive into the real estate business in the first place; and to my mentor, Paul, who pushed me.

INTRODUCTION

I want to give you my brain.

Have you ever wished you could "download" the wisdom, life experience, skill set, or know-how of an expert? This happens to me every time I watch a kung fu movie or see a fighter jet blow past at 800 mph. I think, "Wow. What a rush. I wish I could just download *that* guy's brain, Matrix-style, and do *that*." It also happens every time I see some jerk with a six-pack at the gym: "I don't know what he's doing, or how he finds the grit to *keep* doing it, but I'd like to download *that*."

I don't know squat about six packs or fighter jets or kung fu. I am a real estate expert. In the next few chapters, I will tell you what YOU need to know to think like a real estate expert. Whether you are buying your first home, learning to invest in real estate, or starting your own career as an agent, the 7 strategies in this book will put you well on your way to avoiding classic missteps, acting with knowledge-based confidence, and *enjoying* real estate transactions rather than stressing over them.

I love real estate. It has been good to me—a source of wealth and happiness. My kids owe their diapers and their college funds to it. Much like Chris Hemsworth getting washboard abs, buying and selling a house is no big deal for me because I know what I'm doing. After reading the next few chapters, it won't be a big deal to you either, because you'll know what you're doing. You'll know how to get out of your own way. You'll understand the order of operations in a real estate transaction from finding a lender to closing the deal. You will know how to work with an agent. You will understand your power and role as the buyer, and you will know the right questions to ask. You will know how to dodge the landmines that frequently arise, and how to do so without being a jerk. In short, you'll know how to think like I do

I'm going to give you my brain.

WHO THIS BOOK IS FOR

There are two types of people in the world: *my kind of people*, and *not my kind of people* (Actually, if you count Yankee's fans, there are *three* types, but let's not go there.)

HERE'S WHAT I MEAN:

IMAGINE you are a middle-aged fat guy, and your doctor just told you that you're pre-diabetic. To avoid developing full-blown diabetes, he says, "You are going to have to make some lifestyle changes."

Now, do you,

- (a) Tell him to take a hike?
- (b) Blame the doctor for your problems and demand that *he* fix them?

- (c) Take responsibility and follow his advice?

IF YOU CHOSE (C), you are my kind of person. If you chose (a), went home, binged watched your favorite Netflix show, put away a whole meat-lovers pizza and three beers, felt sorry for yourself, and *then* chose option (c), you're *really* my kind of person.

YOU REALIZE that if you want to change your life and attain some big goal like losing weight (or buying a house), information is power. You don't want to be kept in the dark. You want to find the better way. You want to make your own decisions, and make them in the best way possible. If this sounds like you then you have come to the right place.

2

ABOUT ME, THE AUTHOR

A Bit about Me:

MY NAME IS J.P. Fluellen, and although I now enjoy an epic mohawk and a flourishing career helping people buy and sell homes, I wasn't always a real estate agent. In fact, like many folks in this business, my journey was a colorful and meandering one, with a dream or two that died hard (I'm talking about you, Hollywood). I was born and raised in North Dakota, spent years underperforming in the academic world and doing *okay* in a variety of sales and telemarketing jobs. Along the way, I spent 13 years in the Army National Guard and did a tour in Iraq and Kuwait. Dozens of podcasts, books, classes, and a mentor or two later, I found my calling in real estate, and I haven't looked back since.

ABOUT YOU, THE READER

A Bit About You:

I f you are anything like the average American home buyer:

- You are probably married or in a serious relationship.
- You aren't super rich, or super poor.
- There is a 42% chance you have a college education. (Or, if your college experience was like mine, you got 42% of a college education. Reference pizza and beer).
- There is also a 42% chance you are a first-time homebuyer.
- There is a 79% chance you will use the internet at some point while buying your home (seriously, what the hell are the other 21% doing?).
- There is a 75% chance that you will use a real estate agent while buying your home (and a 25%

chance that you'll be frustrated because you didn't).

- You will spend about four months looking for a home. Less, after reading this book.
- There is a 30% chance you will find the home-buying experience rewarding (lucky for you, this number goes waaaayyyyy *up* after reading this book).
- There is a 60% chance you will regret the way you purchased your first home (lucky for you, this number goes waaaayyyy *down* after reading this book).

IF YOU ARE anything like the people I meet day to day, buying a house is probably an intimidating or challenging prospect. You were probably renting, or living with your parents up to now. You may be freaking out about the amount of responsibility that comes with home ownership, and worried about the mysterious and complicated process of buying a home. Not to worry. Let me pull aside the curtain for you and reveal this process. I'm happy to say that this is a pretty short book and that in an hour or two (or *three*, if you got that 42% college edjumacation), your temporary ignorance will have been cured, you will be feeling much better about life, and you'll be excited about this new chapter you are beginning...

HACK #1

Get Out of Your Own Way.

Before entering the sacred temple, ancient Greeks were admonished, "know thyself." Similarly, when I deployed to Iraq, my dad told me not to be a Jackass and get myself killed. In other words, when you set out on a big journey—and let's face it, buying a house is kind of a big journey—it pays to take a moment of intro-spection and be real with yourself. If you aren't honest with yourself and don't form realistic expectations about buying a home, you will end up getting in your own way throughout the process. Similarly, if you don't overcome a couple common fears before you set out on this journey, you may end up falling on your face.

CASE IN POINT

Jack and Jill (not their real names) were looking for a house with a view. Preferably one on a hill. Problem was, they had no idea how much money they wanted to spend, or whether they wanted that hill to be in the middle of town or two hours out of town. They also didn't know if they were comfortable doing some remodeling, if they needed an extra bedroom for a future kid, if garage space was important, or even whether this home would ever become an investment property for them. After seeing five homes, they weren't sure if the hill was really that important after all. They were also worried about buying an older home where something might *break* someday. Eventually, they bought a five-bedroom townhouse because it was brand new, had a sweet pool and access to a 24hr racquetball court. They thought, "Maybe we can finally get fit, and since it is so new, we shouldn't have any major maintenance problems." However, the place was really too big for them, stretched their budget too much (have you heard the term 'house poor') and didn't have that view they wanted in the first place. Six months later, they were looking to move.

THAT'S what happens when you don't get out of your own way. This is what happens when you (1) aren't real with yourself, and (2) don't overcome common fears that hold homebuyers back. Let's talk about these two things in a bit more detail:

Get Real (Part 1)
Know what you want

THE FIRST STEP to buying a home is figuring out what you

want. Are you looking for an investment property so you can rent out the basement and help pay your mortgage? Is this house a stepping stone to a bigger house in the future, or will this be your '*forever home*'? Do you need to be near good schools? How important is it to be in a quiet neighborhood? How do you feel about an attached garage? How much cash do you have to spend on a down payment, and how much debt are you comfortable with taking on?

SOME OF THESE questions are more important than others, and this is by no means an exhaustive list. The important thing is to think about stuff like this *now*. If you are going through this process with a partner, this section will give you conversation points. You don't have to have all the answers, but you should have a few important ones. The truth is, throughout the home buying process more questions inevitably arise, and you will be forced to reevaluate your priorities. When that happens, remember this section. For now, here is a list of *important* things to consider:

- Are you going to be here long term or short term?
- Do you want to be in the country or in town?
- Is this a second home? Does that change the way you are looking at this purchase?
- What state do you really want to live in?
- How far away from things is *too* far away from things? Work? Groceries? Be serious now...
- Proximity to Schools: This is a two-edged sword. If the school is a factor, then you want to buy a home in a good school district, but sometimes living in a certain school district comes at a premium. I've had clients buy homes they

couldn't afford, just to be in the school district they wanted.

- Do you want to be close to a highway?
- Do you want to be far away from a power plant or refinery?
- Do you want to be close to your in-laws?
- Do you want a condo or a townhouse so you have an HOA to take care of maintenance?
- Do you need enough space to house an elderly family member or other relative at some point?
- Do you want an older home with *"character"*, or a newer home without asbestos?
- Are you comfortable with remodeling? How comfortable? How much remodeling?
- Does it matter if it's an older owner-occupied home versus a foreclosure?
- Do you want something that is new construction with lots of upgrades?
- Are you okay with paying a premium to get exactly what you want? (location comes into play a lot here)
- Are you putting yourself in "location jail" by making decisions based on your kid's school? Are you okay with that? (Think long term, not short term, kids will move out someday and their drama will fade. Maybe...)

HERE IS a list of *less important* things to consider:

- Bedrooms: How many do you really want/need. How big is your bedroom furniture? Do you really need a guest bedroom? If this your first home, maybe you don't.

- Bathrooms: How many kids do you have? More specifically, how many *girls* do you have? Think I'm joking? I have 3 daughters, a son, and a wife, and I can tell you this is a serious matter. How many drawers and other storage space will you need to store all the stuff your family uses in the bathroom? How many bathrooms do you need to stay sane? How many sinks? Showers? Tubs? Toilets?

- Main floor master: Is this a priority? If you need to lose a few pounds and don't mind running up and down stairs, wonderful. On the other hand, if you have bad knees, you know what I'm talking about.

- Main floor laundry: Again important for non-stair people, but also convenient in general. How much time do you spend doing laundry? If your life is anything like mine, this is a surprisingly important room. Keep in mind that even if the laundry is on the main floor, it may be in a high traffic area, like a hallway or kitchen. How does that impact your laundry life?

- Flooring: Do you prefer hardwood, tile, carpet, laminate, vinyl? Certain flooring in certain rooms?

- Layout/Style: Do you like open concept design? Do you want a formal dining room? Do you hate split levels? Do you love walk-out basements?

- Bedroom Size: I have bedrooms on this list twice, because it's worth thinking about twice. A lot of people *don't* make decisions based on bedroom size, and then regret it later. Asleep or not, you are going to spend about half your life in there...

- Yard: Do you want a big yard? Do you need a corner lot? Do you like to mow lawns? Do like to water them? Do you want a sprinkler system? Do you want to pay for someone else to take care of your yard? Will you need a fence and can you afford to put one in if it's not there already? Do you need room for a swing set, a garden? Do you want fancy landscaping?
- Garages: Do you need one? Do you need *three*? How big does it need to be? What are you going to put in there? Motorcycles, 4-wheelers, a classic car that needs two feet of space around it as a safety cushion? Do you want to not only park your minivan in your garage but also get *out* afterward?
- Outbuilding/Barn: Do you have horses? Or perhaps need a large workplace? Does it need to be heated? Do you need extra storage? Do you need a riding arena, or pasture land?
- Views: What do you want to see when you look out the back window?

<u>Get Real (Part 2)</u>
What you want VS Reality

NOW THAT YOU know what you want, I have a bomb to drop on you:

You can't always have what you want.

FOR EXAMPLE, you may decide that you want a well cared for, move-in ready 30-50 year old ranch style brick home on a 1 acre lot, for under $120,000. That's great, but you can't have it. You *definitely* can't have it in Southern California, or within 100 miles of New York City.

INEVITABLY, you are going to have to change what you want to fit into what is possible in the world of rational human beings. Every situation is different. For you, it might mean that to stay under budget you need to consider an older home that needs remodeling. Or it might mean that your budget needs to grow.

THIS IS a moment when a good Real Estate Agent can come in handy (we will talk more about how to find a real estate agent soon, so stay tuned). They will be knowledgeable about what is realistically available in your area, and at what price range. Sometimes it's not fun to hear that what you want is unattainable, but the truth is, this realization gets you a step closer to getting a house, which is what you really want. Often we must compromise, and bring what we want into agreement with what is possible. This is something an agent can guide you in.

THE TYPES of compromises that have to be made here vary widely, but here is a list of common issues and compromises that I see:

- *This house is in my price range(ish):* Looking at homes you can't afford, and then trying to lowball the seller and talk them down to your price range. Sometimes people ask me to do this, but it really is just plain silly. The chance of this working is worse than winning the Powerball Lotto, it wastes all our time and ticks off sellers. The only time you should find yourself in a situation like this is if you are a professional flipper looking at a distressed property, in which case you probably aren't reading this book.

- *Mommy and Daddy's house:* Wanting to buy a house like the one your parents live in versus realizing that they're living in their 4th house and you may need to start smaller, just like they did. You might even have to work multiple jobs for 30 years to afford something big and nice, just like they did. Go figure.

- *Getting what you deserve:* Since there are pictures and numbers everywhere, and you have friends with nice houses, you may think that you *deserve* a 4-bed 3-bath home with hardwood floors, a fireplace, and granite countertops (built in the last 10 years of course). And since you qualified for a $190,000 loan you may feel like you *deserve* to find your dream house listed for $187,000. What? You can't find it? But that's not fair! Well, as Grandpa Jim used to say, "fair is where you go to see the pigs."

- *Buying your dream home:* If you're buying your first home, guess what? You're NOT buying your dream home (Unless you're a billionaire trust fund baby, in which case you've already bought your dream home and you're currently lounging by your pool, sipping something expensive, imaging what next expensive thing you are going to buy, and *not* reading this book. We all loathe you, by the way).

Overcome Common Fears

ANYONE THAT HAS TRIED JUMPING off a high diving board, climbing a ladder, asking a pretty girl out on a date, or snowboarding on stolen Burger King trays while clinging to the back of a moving truck (What? You haven't done that?) will know that fear can keep you from getting what you want. In the story previously mentioned about Jack and Jill, they were afraid of responsibility and the unknown. This kept them from getting a home that would have made them happy in the long run. Similarly, if you don't confront the common fears/excuses of home ownership, you're going to get in your own way.

Now, I don't know what fears or excuses you have specifically, but I bet you will find some of them in the list below, because I see them again and again with my clients. *Especially* first time homebuyers. I promise I'm not going to go all Dr. Phil on you, but take a minute to review the list. See which fears you might be feeling, and then get over it.

· · ·

How do you get over it? I have no idea. As far as home buying goes, it's good enough to just become aware that you have a fear, and consciously decide not to let that fear influence your decisions. Objectivity is what you are after here, so take a look at these common fears and excuses, and see what resonates:

- *It's not the right time: Duh.* There *is* no right time to buy a house. Just like it's rarely a great time to pop the question to your fiancee, have kids, move out of your parent's basement, go on a diet, or start investing in the stock market. The best time to buy a house (or shares in Google) was 20 years ago. The second best time is today. Maybe you think you can't afford a house, and maybe you are right. If you are unemployed, uneducated, unskilled, and have $9 to your name, you can't afford a house. For everyone else, it's pretty doable. If you are saying to yourself, "I'll wait till I have a better job" or "I'll wait till I've saved up more money"- well...Dude! You never save up! There are plenty of programs to assist you in getting into a home, and a good mortgage broker will know them all (more on choosing a lender later). If you can afford to pay rent consistently, you can probably afford to pay a mortgage payment instead, and you might as well not be throwing all that money away with nothing to show for it.
- *Interest rates are too high:* Interest rates are always changing. You wouldn't stop driving just because gas prices go up, would you? In the 1980's interest rates were 21%. When I bought my first home,

interest rates were 6.975%, and I thought *that* was good. Interest rates aren't forever, and you can always refinance later if they drop.

- *I'm not ready to grow up:* When I was growing up, I thought that I had to graduate from college, find the perfect job, get married, and have 2.5 kids before I could buy a house. The fact of the matter is you are usually better off the earlier you begin. True, you may have become comfortable relying on your dad, or the landlord to pay for/fix stuff when it breaks. But you'll figure it out. Dad did. And you will feel great doing it. True, you will have less disposable income paying a $1200 mortgage payment than you do paying a $1100 rent payment, but you will also have something to show for it. You will be building equity. You will be putting money in your own pocket.

- *I can live in my parent's basement forever:* I see this all the time. Come on now...If you make livable wages and live at home, do your parents a favor and get your own place as soon as you can. I have told my kids (and they're all under 12 at the time of this book) that they need to begin planning their exit strategy NOW! You think I joke? When parents fail to set their kids up for success in this way, they fail their kids. Period. If you're in this situation, it's time to get out.

- *Renting is easier:* Throwing your money in the trash is easy too, but you don't see the garbage guy carrying around bags of cash. Yes, renting is easier (or at least *simpler*), sort of, but it's usually not the best thing for you. When you buy a home, you start to get ahead. You put a little

money away every month when you pay your
mortgage, and meanwhile your home increases
in value.

IF READING the list of common fears helped, here are my top
5 reasons to buy a house *now*:

1. *Life Change:* If you're looking for a house, chances
   are you had a life change recently. Your family
   got bigger. You bought a dog. You have a kid on
   the way and you need more space. You realized
   that renting sucks. You got a new job. You're sick
   of living at home. You want more freedom and
   control over your environment ("I want my
   bedroom to be PURPLE, gosh darnit!). Whatever
   your reasons, hold onto them and think
   frequently about how awesome it will be when
   you get to the other side of this journey.
2. *Opportunity:* Money + Time = Opportunity. No
   matter how you slice it, it costs money to have a
   roof over your head. Year after year, you will
   either pay that money to your landlord, and he
   will invest it or bank it (creating more
   opportunity in *his* life); or you will pay that
   money to your mortgage lender, and eventually
   you will own your own home (creating more
   opportunity in *your* life).
3. *Leverage:* That opportunity you created for
   yourself looks like this: after 5 years of making
   mortgage payments, instead of owning nothing
   (which would be the case if you had been

renting) you now own 15%, or 25%, or 30%, of the value of your home. Meaning that you effectively have $25k, $50k, or $70k in the bank that you would not have had otherwise. Now, you can sell your home and buy a new house that is $70k more expensive. Or you can refinance to a lower interest rate and keep paying down your mortgage, looking forward to the day that you will live rent-free. Instead of throwing away the cost of living, you leverage it to better your life and increase your assets.

4. *You got kicked out:* If your parents are like mine were, they always give you crap for making more money than they did, and keep telling you to get your own place, start paying, or go to school. Best way to shut them up (I mean, *honor their wishes)*: Buy your own home.

5. *Divorce:* Let's be real here. You don't want to go back to renting after you've been living in a house. I can hear you from here: Life sucks, you're depressed, and you've got 13 kids to pay child support for. Still, let's not go backward.

HACK #2

Work WITH Your Agent

We will discuss in some detail later how to select a real estate agent, but how do you work with one effectively?

My main tip for you is to get educated. The more educated you are about the process of buying a house, the better your relationship with your agent will be. Then, instead of relying on your agent to be the expert at all times, you can have a more balanced working relationship. This is important, considering the amount of time you are going to spend together. Learn something, and be a useful part of the team! If you have a working knowledge of the subject, you will also be able to accurately assess whether your agent is doing a good job or not. The good news is, this book is part of that education process I'm talking about.

· · ·

IF YOU ARE THE BUYER, there is literally no reason NOT to work with an agent, because generally, the seller will be covering the agent's fee. Why would you not want to take advantage of an expert's advice? By the way, work with an agent that *you* choose. It's not enough for you to work with the seller's agent. You need your own. You want your agent to be motivated to make *you* happy, and have *your* best interest in mind, rather than just wanting to close the deal and make his/her money.

IF YOU ARE THE SELLER, you're going to be paying the agent a pretty penny. Use your agent! Why would you pay for someone's help if you are not going to take advantage of it? Listen to your agent, and then take their advice. You're not paying him/her just so you can ignore them.

YOU SHOULD KNOW that when you start working with an agent, there will be some paperwork involved. One of the first things you will sign is a Buyer/Broker Agreement (it goes by different names. In Wyoming, for example, we call it a Buyer's Agency Agreement). This is an employment agreement between you and the agent, and comes with a time accord (usually 3 or 6 months), stating that you will work with the agent, and that the agent will get paid when you buy a house. This is important for the agent, because they work for free until you buy.

> PRO TIP: *Don't sign the Buyer/Broker Agreement until you know for sure that you've found the right agent.*

ABOVE ALL ELSE, make sure you get an agent that you like, and then lean on him or her throughout the process. All corniness aside, an agent really IS the person that keeps the home-buying process from being lonely, confusing, or intimidating, but it only works if you allow him to do so. Make sure you are clear about your questions, desires, and expectations regarding your house.

REAL ESTATE AGENTS tend to wear many hats during the process of buying a house—expert witness, life coach, financial advisor, friend, marriage counselor—so it is important important to let your agent know about any and all problems and questions up front. The earlier the better! If you want more "hand holding" (in-person meetings, extra time at viewings, etc.), just let your agent know! In actual fact, your agent is *not* your best friend or drinking buddy (nor would you want your drinking buddies to help you find a house—reference the movie, *Animal House*), but you *still* need to communicate well with them.

HACK #3

Understand Your Power

Have you ever seen that old black and white movie, *12 Angry Men*? It's about a murder trial. 11 out of the 12 jurors voted guilty right away, and were eager to deliver their verdict and get on with their lives, but 1 guy (Juror #8, played by Henry Fonda) disagrees. What looked like a quick decision, grinds to a screeching halt as everyone is forced to re-evaluate. In the story, Juror #8 understood his power. It happens to be the same power that *you* have as the buyer in a real estate transaction: You have a voice, and nothing is going to happen until you are on board. Remember, the seller *wants* to sell the house; provided you are courteous and reasonable, they will likely be willing to jump through a hoop or two to get you on board. They will certainly be willing to answer your questions, let you have one more look at the house, etc.

HERE ARE some questions you might ask:

- What is the motivation level of the seller?
- Is there room for negotiation on the price?
- Why is the seller moving? Are they staying in town, buying another home? Moving out of state? Is it a divorce situation? Is someone moving into a nursing home?
- How long have they owned the property?
- What is the average utility bill?
- Are there any other offers on the home?
- How long has it been on the market?
- Have there been any recent price changes?
- Is there a property disclosure?
- Has the seller done any repairs or improvements since they have owned the home?
- Would the seller be willing to do_____(something you want fixed, perhaps?) before closing?

No one is going to ignore your questions in this situation. No one is going to ignore you. *You* are the fish that the seller is trying to catch. This is your power.

HACK #4

Ask the Right Questions

You will (or should) have many, many questions during the home buying process.

Ask them all!

We aren't in the fourth grade anymore, too shy to raise our hand because we're sitting next to Susie Steeples. We aren't in college either, afraid that our question is dumb and hoping someone *else* will ask it so that we don't have to. No one else will ask your questions for you. And remember: there are no dumb questions!

Check that. There *are* dumb questions, but you have to ask

them anyway. Otherwise your knowledge won't grow, and as we all know, the only thing worse that dumb questions, is a dumb person.

I ONCE KNEW a couple (we'll call them Jack and Jill) who made an offer on an older home and decided to NOT ask any questions. They were first time home buyers, and they thought their agent (call him Bill) could read minds (Earth to Spock. Come in, Spock!). Bill, incapable of vulcan mind melds, did his best. He arranged for plumbing, electrical, roof, and sewer line inspections. The receipt for said inspections arrives, and Bill, trying to simplify things for Jack and Jill, tacks the inspection cost onto the closing statement so that his buyers don't have to write multiple checks. Of course, when it comes time to write said check, both Jack and Jill are surprised by the higher amount, and suddenly don't have enough money for the down payment. Bill coughs up money for the inspections, because he is uber compassionate and doesn't want Jack and Jill to live on a hill.

OF COURSE, that wasn't very fair to Bill. And, if you didn't notice, it all happened because of a breakdown in communications. Don't let it happen to you!

WHILE YOU'RE ASKING questions and practicing good communications skills (which, if you didn't notice are the subject of Hacks 2-4), be sure that you ask the *right* questions. The tricky thing is, the *right* questions can vary from house to house. Essentially, the right questions are the obvious questions. The questions that, if you fail to ask them, will get you into trouble. For example, I once sold a house with three sump pumps in it. *Three.* Now, what are the right questions in this situation?

HOW ABOUT: *Why* are there THREE sump pumps? Does this house have water problems?

USE YOUR HEAD! Think smart! Hopefully, your agent will think to ask the right questions, but if he forgets, it's on you. It's your house. You're the one that has to live in it, so ask the right questions. That's about all there is to hack #4. However, it occurs to me that apart from the obvious questions, the *right* questions, there are some other important questions that people frequently forget to ask, so I've put together a list of them for you. These are the questions that I see causing the most problems for people when they forget to ask them. Some we have already discussed, and some will be treated more deeply later:

- How much house can we comfortably afford?
- What do we really want?
- Do we really understand what we are getting into?
- Are there any upfront costs?
- What costs are there if we don't close?
- Do we lose our earnest money if we don't close?
- How much do inspections cost and who pays for them?
- Is there a property disclosure form?
- *Ask your insurance agent:* Does the home have a

CLUE report? A CLUE (Comprehensive Loss
Underwriting Exchange) report will show a
history of past insurance claims on your
property. This can help you get more insight into
potential problems or at least *past* issues with the
home. Get a CLUE.

- *Ask the Police:* Where are the hot crime spots in
  your area? Have there been a lot of break-ins on
  your street? Do you have kids? Are any of your
  neighbors registered sex offenders?
- *Ask the internet:* What are school rankings like for
  your area?
- *Ask Facebook:* Do people enjoy living here? Do a
  Facebook poll. Alternatively, you could knock on
  the doors of your potential new neighbors and
  ask them what the neighborhood is like. Find the
  guy who has been living there for 25 years.
  Bonus: if you end up moving in, you've already
  met your neighbors!

REMEMBER, the answers to these questions may or may not
constitute a reason not to buy the house. The important
thing is, you asked, and now you know. Even if you're not
excited about the information you receive, informed decisions are usually the best kind.

HACK #5

Dodge the Landmines

THIS IS the part of the book where I tell a couple scary stories. Cautionary tales, if you will, to instill in you a bit of...well...*caution.* The fact is, sometimes things go wrong. Sometimes people aren't kind-hearted and selfless. Best to realize this now, and be on guard a bit:

ONCE, an unsuspecting new homeowner started a little DIY project and discovered, upon removing a bit of sheetrock, that the wall behind it had been mostly burned away in a fire. The previous owners either never filed an insurance claim at all, or filed one and then spent the money on a new Slurpee machine. They covered it up with a piece of wallboard to hide the damage, and the new guy got shafted. Not very nice. Moral of the story: You can't always *see* the problems. Therefore, get a CLUE report when possible, and poke around to see if past insurance claims were fixed correctly. Here's another story about that:

A HAIL STORM destroyed a roof in Cheyenne WY, so the owners filed an insurance claim, and decided to take that money and fix it *themselves*. This way they might save some money! They even decided to put on a *metal* roof. Never mind that they didn't know *how* to install a metal roof. They slapped one up, and listed the home for sale. Unlike the last one, this story has a happy ending, because the new owner's real estate agent (yours truly) took one look at the botched metal roof and said "Yeah...we're getting that sucker checked for sure." Of course, it didn't pass inspection, and the sellers had to pay to put *another* new roof on (this time installed by professionals). Yeah, they were pissed. But my buyer was happy!

ONCE, I had a client purchase their first home, and later encounter some problems: During the purchase process, they paid for a roof inspection and the roofing company said it looked good. Yet when the spring rains came, the roof leaked bad. My clients called me, I did a bit of mediation for them with the roofing company, and at the end of the day, they were able to compromise on who was responsible for the damage and get some help. See? Sometimes you benefit from communicating with your agent even *after* the home-buying process.

ON ANOTHER OCCASION, I had a homeowner call me complaining of problems with a light switch—it kept popping the breaker, until after a while, resetting the breaker didn't fix the problem any longer. We reached out to the electrical company who did the original inspection, and after some investigation they discovered some aluminum wiring that that they had missed in the original inspection. This company, being reputable and trustworthy, fixed their mistake and replaced the wiring for free. *That* is why you should trust your agent in selecting quality companies to do your inspections.

LANDMINES COME in all shapes and sizes, and they aren't always easy to spot. As in the stories above, you don't find them until after you have purchased the home. After all, if they had big flashing neon signs saying "BEWARE—GIANT MONEY PIT," then they wouldn't be landmines. They'd be casinos. Real estate agents (provided you didn't choose a super green one) may be more adept at spotting these than you are, so listen to your agent! He might just save you $10,000. Beyond that, if something seems wrong, looks wrong, feels wrong, smells wrong, sounds wrong, get to the bottom of it.

9

HACK #6

Don't be a Jerk

YOU'D THINK this goes without saying, but apparently it does not.

THIS HACK IS about how to get along with people in the social environment that is real estate transactions. You've heard of that book, *How to Win Friends and Influence People*, by Dale Carnegie? This is the short version just for buying houses. There is a lot to say, but I've paired it down to the essentials. Watch for some repeating themes in the list below, and you may get a clue as to the most important point.

How to not piss off your agent:

- *Be respectful.* House hunting is full of inconveniences for you (you kind of have to wait on the seller, your agent, and everyone else to get their stuff together before you can go look at a place), but it's also inconvenient for your agent. The best time to work with you is probably after work, when you can bring your family to see the place, but that's *his* family time too. This is, of course, just one example.

- *Know what you want.* From an agent's perspective, there is nothing more frustrating than working with a client who waffles around on what they want, or who just have no clue whatsoever. Don't be that guy! We discussed all this in Hack #1, so hopefully this isn't a problem for you.

- *Commit.* Eventually, you are going to have to commit to something. Some people forget that. If you don't have this mentality, then at some point, your real estate agent will tire of showing you houses. If you've looked at 30 houses and not made an offer, your agent probably doesn't like you anymore. Also, you might need therapy. Just sayin'.

How to not piss off the seller:

- *Be Respectful.* Remember what I said about repeating themes? Once again, while this process is tough for you, it can be that way for the seller as well. Maybe they are living in the home still, and every time you want to come by and see the house they have to clean it and then get their 4 kids and their dogs out before you get there, and then go hang out at the park or visit the Wendy's drive thru for the 17th time this month while they wait for you to stop walking around their house and peeking in their closets ("Honey, did you check the bathroom after Max finished in there? Ahh, sh**!"). It can be frustrating for everyone, so just chill out, be respectful of people's time, and embrace the process.

- *Show Up.* Once again, showing a house is a bit of a production for the seller (and your agent, by the way). Among other things, people have rearranged their schedules for you. So freaking show up! 'Nough said.
- *Don't be a lowballer.* What do I mean by this? Maybe this scene will illustrate my point:

Seller: Asking price on the house is $195,000.
Buyer: (Spits tobacco in the dirt and tucks thumbs behind suspenders) I'll give yeh' 50 bucks for it.
J.P. Fluellen: (Jumps out from behind a bush and slaps buyer in the face) Did you even *READ* my book, you dumb@$$?!

Okay, so that is a drastic example. No one is going to offer .0002% of the asking price, and I would (probably) never jump out from behind a bush and slap someone. Unless they deserved it. But come on now, talk to your agent about your offer price and take their advice. If you offer less than asking, have a good reason for it. Only a fool offers the asking price (without a good reason), and only a fool offers less (without a good reason).

RECAP

If you haven't noticed, most of the tips in this section really boil down to being courteous and respectful. A real estate transaction can be a frustrating process for everyone, so just chill out, be respectful of people's time, and embrace the process. And remember, Hack #6 becomes *more* important when things go wrong. It's easy to be nice when everything is rainbows and fairy hearts. But when the crap hits the fan —when something goes wrong with the transaction, when the house appraises weird, or the inspectors find some large-scale flaw, or whatever, *that* is when you are likely to be disrespectful and piss people off...

Don't.

HACK #7

Order of Operations

BUYING a house is akin to doing one of those painfully complex seventh grade math problems: intimidating at first glance, and difficult unless you know the trick of it—the *order of operations*. Remember those? Multiply *before* you subtract. Divide before you add. Elucidate before you extrapolate...unless ducks are involved...or something like that. Okay, so I don't know much about mathematical orders of operations. But I *do* know the order of operations for buying a house, and stepping you through them is a highly effective way of familiarizing you with the whole process from start to finish. I will break down—simply—every important step of buying a house, in order of how it happens in the real world. If you happen to be selling instead of buying, the steps will be much the same. Strap in, though. This is by far the longest hack, and there is a lot to cover. Here we go:

Step 0
Decide you want to buy a house

Step 1
Determine the Sale Type

SOME COMMON TYPES of home sales are: For sale by owner (FSBO), As is where is, and owner occupied homes.

FSBO's

DON'T EVER BUY AN FSBO. Doing so is much like acting as your own attorney in a court of law: just because it's legal doesn't mean it's a good idea. There is more to buying a home than picking a shiny one off the shelf, and real estate professionals are familiar with this many-faceted process. You might be the DIY type, but this is a great time to shelve that aspect of your personality and avail yourself of professional help. You'll thank me later. This is especially true if you have not owned a home (or three) before. If this is your first time, you won't have good instincts about whether you are being treated fairly or not. You won't have a sense of when there might be "bodies in the walls"— details that should be disclosed, but are being covered up. If you are a super savvy individual with some real life experience and a highly tuned BS meter, *and* previous experience buying and selling homes, you can maybe ignore me on this point. *Maybe*. Still, do so at your own peril...

As is Where is

THIS IS a home that the seller will not make any changes or corrections to. You can find some really good deals in this category, but be careful; when someone is selling something "as is" there is usually a reason. With homes of this type, you may be allowed to do inspections prior to purchasing, but whatever is unearthed during such inspections will simply be for your information; you have no leverage to get the current owner to change things. That said, since the majority of these properties come with a particular set of challenges, there are cases in which the seller may allow for a due diligence clause in the contract, which gives the buyer (you) a way to cancel the contract and back out if you suddenly realize you're in over your head.

MANY *As is Where is* properties are bank owned, or REO (Real Estate Owned—meaning owned by some sort of real estate entity) properties, in which case they may be listed as such because the seller just doesn't have the time or resources to dink around with repairs and the like. In this case, you might find some good buys. Other properties may be owned by sellers that are simply trying to avoid paying for requested or required repairs and the like. If you have a competent agent to craft a good contract for you, you might be able to persuade sellers to forgo their *As is Where is* label and move on. After all, sellers want to sell.

OWNER OCCUPIED HOMES

THIS BASICALLY MEANS that someone bought the home and lived in it. They may still live in it, or they may have moved on, but they still own it and are motivated to sell. This is probably what you are looking for. It's also the majority of what is out there. The remainder of this book deals primarily with this type of sale.

<u>Step 2</u>
Financing

IF YOU HAVE $300,000 carefully stashed away in your old Batman lunchbox, you're set. No doubt there will be one savvy dude that reads this who is in this position. For the rest of us, it's time to choose a lender.

NOW, you may think it's odd to get financing before you start looking at houses, but nothing could be further from the truth. It's okay to go window shopping at the mall, but imagine walking into the Cartier Botique on the Avenue des Champs-Élysées in Paris, striding up to the counter, pointing at a $40,000 watch and saying, "Hey dude, I wanna try that one, and that one, and then that one," and then walking out without buying anything...you're going to piss people off right? (Mind you, they're French, so there is a solid chance they were pissed off already). Buying houses is kind of like that. People will take you seriously if you show up to look with financing already taken care of. Otherwise, you will be wasting their time, and they'll know it. Also, you will avoid getting frustrated or burned out by the process of looking. Don't look much until you are ready to put your money where your mouth is.

WHAT IS A LENDER?

A LENDER IS (DUH, I know) someone who fronts the money for your home purchase. They buy the house for you, and then over the next 15-30 years you pay them back the cost of the house, plus interest. It all plays out much like when I bought my first car:

You: Dad that car is *sweet*. I want to buy it, but it's $5,000.
Dad: How much do you have?
You: $500.
Dad: (Evil laughter) Tell you what. Give me that $500 right now and I'll buy it for you and let you drive it around, but I'll keep the title. Then you can pay me $500 every month for the next year and a half. After that, it's yours."
You: But, that means I'll pay like $9,000 in the end instead of $5,000! That's totally unfair!
Dad: Okay, buy it yourself then. Good luck, Mr. Five Hundred Bucks.
You: (considering your options) Damn...

IN THIS CASE, Dad is the lender. In the real estate world, the word "lender" refers to both the *Originator,* which is the real live person you will be dealing with, *and* the institution they work for that actually foots the bill.

THINGS TO CONSIDER when choosing a lender

- Fees: Not all lenders charge the same fees, and the cost differential can be a big one, so ask some questions to understand what you're getting into. Some lenders charge a flat fee. Some charge a percentage of the purchase price.
- History and Specialty: Just because you've been banking at Joe Blow's Butkickin' Bank since you were 18, and you have a credit card with them, it doesn't mean they will be the best people to help you buy a house. Some lenders are not as knowledgeable or efficient as others. This is often true when comparing standard banks (who do a bit of everything) to mortgage companies (who specialize in nothing but mortgage lending, and are therefore very good at it).
- Underwriting: In a lending institution, the *underwriters* are the mysterious bearded old men who sit in high towers at undisclosed locations, looking over your personal information and loan application, and deciding whether or not to lend you the money. Seriously though, they are the decision makers, and generally, you will not meet them personally (because they don't want to be swayed by your cute face, or have their car egged if they decide not to give you money). Rather, you

will work with a loan officer, who acts as a go-
between for you and the underwriters. Some
lenders have underwriters that live halfway
across the world and speak only native Swahili.
This can be a bit of a problem. Usually, it is easier
to work with a lender that does their *own*
underwriting, in house, or at least has someone
local do it. This is a good thing to ask about ("Do
you do your own underwriting?").

- Street Cred: Ask your real estate agent to suggest
  one or two lenders to you. Generally, they will
  have worked with a couple that stand out from
  the crowd. These should be lenders that get
  things done on time, and are easy to work with.
- Physical Presence: It's okay to meet online, but
  eventually the relationship has to get physical,
  you know? If you go with a totally online lender,
  your agent better know them well. Just sayin'.
- Loan Types Offered: Ask your lender what types
  of loans they offer, and what would be best for
  your situation. You want to go with a lender
  who knows their stuff, and is in a position to
  help you with a VA (Veteran's Administration. If
  you are military, or retired military, this is
  probably for you) FHA (First Time Home Buyer.
  If you are buying your first house in several
  years, you can get sweet rates and low down
  payments with this type of loan), Rural
  Development (Special rates if you are buying a
  place in the middle of nowhere), or a
  Conventional loan (regular home loan, in which
  you will be required to have 5%-20% of the cost
  of the house before you buy). If you ask about

one of these and your lender doesn't know what you are talking about, or doesn't have a firm opinion about which is best for you, go elsewhere.

PRO TIP: *A note about VA loans. Banks will often tell you that if you choose to go with a VA loan, you* have *to do it through* their *bank. Not true! The same goes with relocation companies.*

Pre-qualification

WHEN IT COMES time to find an agent and go shopping for houses, the most important tool in your belt is the prequalification letter. This is, essentially, the document a lender writes up saying how much money you are good for. In other words, how much they are going to lend you to buy a house; the prequal letter proves your eligibility to actually buy a home, as well as what price bracket you will be looking in. Looking for homes without a prequal letter in your pocket is like driving without a license: doable, but stupid. Without a prequal letter, you will not know how much house you can afford, and you will be unable to make an offer on a home, or start the buying process.

WHEN YOU FIRST MEET WITH your lender, they will begin the

process of prequalifying you for a loan. As part of this process they will need from you some or all of the following:

- 2 years of tax returns
- Your last 2 months bank statements
- At least 1 pay stub
- A 2 year work history
- Other documentation regarding current debts or other assets
- In general, written, official evidence that your debt to income ratio is under 43% or so. In other words, if you make $100 a month (for the sake of easy math), your lender will want to make sure that after you pay your credit card bill, your car payment, and your mortgage payment, you'll still have 60 bucks left to live on.

RANDOM STUFF YOU SHOULD KNOW:

- If overtime pay is an integral part of your income, they will want to see a long history of it to prove consistency.
- Retirement or social security income may be used to qualify you if you have been collecting for 3 or more years. Same thing with Alimony or child support: you can use it if you have been receiving for at least 3 months, and will continue to receive for at least 3 years.
- Rental income may also be used to qualify you, so long as you can demonstrate stable income on tax returns.

AFTER YOU ARE PREQUALIFIED for a loan, don't screw it up. Think of it as getting engaged. Rather, now is a REALLY bad time to open a new line of credit, quit your job, buy a new car, invest $50k in the stock market, or generally purchase *anything* that you can't pay cash for (In other words, it's a bad time to go flirt with your old girlfriend).. Just be stable for a while. Any major financial moves you make between the time you are prequalified and the time your loan is written will be scrutinized by your lender. What's that you say? Your brother owes you $7,000 and wants to write you a check now? Well unless he wants to sign some forms and have a conversation with your lender proving that he is not secretly giving you cash to help buy a house, he should wait a couple months. Be stable. Be smart. Be boring for a few weeks.

COMMON SENSE AND *SELF*-PREQUALIFICATION: I would be remiss if I didn't stop now to talk a bit about common sense, and how you, as a responsible human being, should prequalify *yourself* when it comes to buying a house. More important than whether you can convince a lender to spot you $300k, is ensuring that *you* are ready to take on this type of financial obligation. If, for example, I gave you $50, and 24 hours later you have no idea where it went or what you spent it on, it may be time to read a couple books, brush up on good financial habits for a few months, and come back to this whole home buying process after your financial IQ goes up a couple points. Above all, this is the concept that you should understand and live by: If you don't have it, don't spend it. This is particularly important to live by now, because in buying a house, you are about to spend a BUNCH of money you don't have. *Yet.* The truth is, you will have that money eventually, and you are just paying it off in small chunks. That's doable for a house. If, however, you are spending a bunch of money you don't have in other aspects of your life as well, you are going to run into trouble.

TO THE SELF-EMPLOYED: If you are self-employed, you may have a harder time than the rest of us getting a loan. For whatever reason, when you have a traditional job, a lender is satisfied by one paycheck from an employer as grounds to spot you hundreds of thousands of dollars. But if you are self-employed, they want you to prove your income for the last 25 years (Just kidding. It's like 2 or 3). *And* they can only use your *net* income to qualify you. Sucks huh? Yes, there are challenges. For tips on self-employment in general, and also specifically as it relates to preparing to buy a home, I highly recommend the book, *Profit First*, by Mike Michalowicz. A good lender, and a CPA can give you further counsel.

OKAY, you've met with a lender, done a bunch of paperwork, and had your wallet inspected. You have a prequalification letter in your hand and you're ready to rock. It's time to get an agent.

Step 3
Real Estate Agents

IN ALL REALITY, you might get an agent before you find a

lender. If so, your agent can recommend a lender. If not, your lender will know good agents. Steps 2 and 3 are a bit fluid. At the end of the day, you want a competent, honest professional who has your best interests in mind, who is willing to fight for you, and who you can communicate well with. When you are looking for a person who fits that bill, recommendations from friends and family can be good. However, take the time to interview at least 2 or 3 agents before you decide. You're going to be pretty much married to this person for 4-6 weeks at least, so don't rush in blindly. Here are some things to consider during this process:

- Experience: How long have they been in the business? Experience is great, sometimes. On the other hand, rookie agents can be some of the best to work with simply because they are so motivated, and they want to be very thorough, and make sure they please you.
- Professionalism: Sometimes it's great to have your best friend be your real estate agent. Then again, if he's the wrong kind of guy, it could be the worst decision ever. Does she make herself reasonably available? How long does it take him to call you back? How hard does she work to make sure your needs are met? Does he go out of his way to protect your interests? Does he go above and beyond? Again, make sure you interview you agents for the job. They don't just get it automatically.
- Traits and Personality: Does he smell like fish sticks all the time? Does he have a distracting Mohawk? Does she remind you of your aunt Sheri, whom you *hate*? Is he pushy or

intimidating? These things can seem trivial, but
you need to be very comfortable around this
person, because you will be making big decisions
with them. Pick someone you like, someone who
listens well and is easy to talk to.

- Designations: Real estate agents, like college
graduates, have different designations that
correspond with different levels and types of
education. Find out what they are! Generally, the
more they have, the better.

- Street Cred: Some agents are just going to be
widely known and respected. Some are going to
be widely known for the opposite reason. Ask
around.

<u>Step 4</u>
Shopping (a.k.a. "the fun part")

REMEMBER earlier when you gave a lot of thought to what
type of home you wanted? Now is a good time to share those
thoughts with your agent and let him go to work. Remember, there should and will be some "give and take" in this
process. He may come back to you with some reality checks
about things you want. For example, he might inform you
that you can't check all nineteen boxes on your list of must-
haves while also staying in budget. Or, he might sense your
needs and ask you questions that change your list of desires.
For example, he might say, "I know you are looking for
something with an attached garage, but Property X just
came on the market today that is significantly under budget.
No garage, but you could save money now and build one

later." This type of back and forth is a part of the process. Embrace it.

YOU ARE GOING to see a lot of houses. That's okay. Try to be relaxed. Take your time, and try to visualize yourself living in the space. Chances are, after five or ten houses, you will have a pretty good idea of what you do and don't like, and your agent will too.

HERE ARE some things to remember while shopping for a house:

- Try to enjoy the process. Nobody likes a sourpuss.
- When you find the perfect house and decide it's what you want, you will go through it a few more times. Each time, you will see things you missed before—things you don't like. Each time you view the home, you will see more issues. This is normal. There *is* no perfect house. Don't sweat it. Compromise and home improvement are a part of home ownership. I'm not saying you should settle for less, but if you really like a place, don't be a snob and demand perfection. It doesn't exist anyway.
- Remember that if there is something about the house you don't love, you may have some power to change the situation. If the seller is motivated, they may be willing to pay for changes or fixes. (More on this in step 6.)

Step 5
The Offer

WHEN YOU FINALLY FIND THE home you want to pull the trigger on, you will probably have a moment of terror—or at least mild doubt. This is normal! Get over it. Remember: millions of homes are bought and sold every year, and life goes on. When you are through that, and have decided to commit, it's time to make an offer. Your agent can help you put an offer on the home, and then the seller can accept your offer, reject it, or present you with a counter-offer. For example, if the home is listed at $250,000 perhaps you offer $242,000 and the seller comes back with $245,000.

THINGS TO KNOW ABOUT OFFERS:

- You need to understand whether the market you are buying in is what we call a *seller's* market, or a *buyer's* market. In a *seller's* market, there are many buyers, but few sellers; the seller has the advantage and more power over the price. In a buyer's market, it is the opposite. In a seller's market, your chance (as the buyer) of getting the deal of the century are approximately zero, and there will be little room to negotiate on price. In fact, it's not uncommon in these markets for starting offers to come in $5,000 or $10,000 *over* asking price and for the property to be sold in a matter of days or even hours.
- A lot comes down to timing. Maybe you make

an offer, but you asked to see the home several times first, and your offer is a bit under asking price. Whereas another guy saw the house once and offered the asking price. If he put his offer in first, he'll almost certainly get the house instead of you. If he offered second, he might *still* get the house because he's willing to pay the asking price, and appears easier to work with.

- Representation is important. In other words, use an agent. Let's say you offer a low-ball offer, and the seller counters. Then you decide you are willing to pay more, so you counter their counter. After which the seller realizes you can be persuaded, so he re-counters your counter, and now you are on offer number four. Things get ridiculous fast, and it's moments like this that you want an experienced negotiator in your corner rather than trying to manage the situation yourself. Things can get exciting, and that is exactly when you *don't* want to skip steps or omit needed documentation, etc.

- Once again, *commit.* A seller is more motivated to work with a buyer that seems serious, and commits quickly. If you know you want the house, pull the trigger. If you don't know, move on.

- Read your neighborhood covenants. Neighborhoods have CC&R's or, Covenant's, Conditions and Restrictions that are, in essence, a set of general neighborhood rules regarding the use of land and property. When your offer is accepted, you generally must sign a document

that sates you agree to these rules, so it's nice to
know what you are getting into beforehand.

- Earnest money will influence how the seller
views a buyer. Earnest money is the money
deposited by a buyer at the beginning of the sale
process (paid by personal check) to show that
they are serious. If the buyer backs out, they lose
the earnest money. If the sale goes through, the
earnest money is applied to the down payment.
The earnest money is held by a third party,
generally a title company, until the deal is closed.
How much earnest money should you put down?
It all comes down to your comfort level, and the
recommendations of your agent. However, it is
important to remember that the seller will see
how much earnest money you are willing to put
down when they review your offer, so it WILL
influence their perception of you. As a general
rule, if you want to be taken seriously, you should
put down at least 1% of the purchase price, and
no less than $1,000.

Step 6
Inspections

AFTER THE SELLER accepts your offer, you get to REALLY
take a close look at the home. From now on, it is your due
diligence to ensure that the property you are buying is
exactly what you think it is. You will pay for the inspections,
because you want the inspectors to be on your side, trying to
find problems with the home, rather than hide them. You

want all the dirty little secrets to be exposed at this point. There WILL be issues. That's okay. There is still time to address them. You can ask for the seller to pay for them to be fixed or to adjust the purchase price. The most basic inspection you will get is called a "home inspection." In this, someone will open all your cupboard doors, turn every faucet knob, and flip every light switch etc., then report back to you. You will need a roof inspection, because the roof must be insurable before you can get a loan. You will also get electrical and plumbing inspections. These are the must-haves. Above and beyond these, you order inspections for whatever your little heart desires, including radon (toxic gas), lead (as in lead poisoning), foundation, etc. The one that I often encourage is getting your sewer lines inspected, especially if you are buying an older home.

OTHER THINGS TO know during inspections:

- Consider requesting the buyer to pay for a home warranty at this point. A home warranty is a one-year renewable service contract that pays for expensive repairs on things like appliances, furnace/AC systems, etc. This protects you against situations like your furnace breaking in the middle of winter 3 weeks after you buy your house. It's kind of like having a landlord, and being able to call him up to fix the big stuff. These are highly recommended and will give you great peace of mind. After the first year, you can choose to continue to pay for this service yourself, or drop it.
- Make sure the seller provides you with a

property condition statement. This is a document in which the seller is required to disclose any information about remodeling or structural changes, as well as "latent defects," which are basically problems about which the seller would have knowledge, but which the buyer couldn't be reasonably expected to discover during inspections.

Step 7
Appraisals and Repairs

AT THIS POINT, you will pay for someone to appraise the home, and inspect it for the lender, so that the lender can be sure that they are investing in a decent property and paying an appropriate price for it. Depending on the type of loan you are getting, there may be "lender required repairs" discovered during inspections. These are usually minor things, like peeling paint, lack of downspouts, etc. Generally the seller will be responsible for paying for lender required repairs.

> PRO TIP: *Do NOT give your final move-out notice to your current landlord until the dust has settled in the inspections/repair process of your new home. This is a phase where things can go sideways and the deal can fall through. If it does, it's pretty embarrassing to go back to your landlord and be like "Uh, you know how I said I was going to move out this week? Yeah...can I stay?"*

Step 8
Final Walk Through

MAKE sure you do a final walk through right before closing, to make sure nothing strange has happened or changed. If, for example the seller has been living in the home during the offer and inspections, and moves out a couple days before closing, you might walk through the house right before closing and discover that they have been using a wardrobe to hide a giant hole in the wall. If you discover things like this *before* you buy, you have leverage to make the seller address them. If you discover them *after* you buy, it's your problem (unless you want to get a lawyer). Make sure all the repairs were actually done, and are complete. Also, this is a good time to address home cleanliness. The home should be move-in ready. Did they leave it a mess? Will you have to deep-clean for 19 hours before you can set your stuff down? Make sure it's ready for you. Go online and search for a final walk through checklist, or ask your agent to provide you with one.

Step 9
Closing

I ONCE HAD a client ask me if they had to show up to closing. YES! You have to show up! The closing will happen at the title company, or at the lender's office, and representatives from all parties must attend. At this meeting, you will sign a bunch of paperwork (and I *mean* a bunch), and you will leave with the keys to your new house! How cool is that?

HERE ARE some things you should know about closing:

- If you have an awesome agent, they will give you a cool gift at closing. If they don't give you a gift, they aren't awesome.
- As part of closing, you will purchase title insurance. Title insurance ensures YOU, the buyer, against any strange or weird things that can happen with titles. For example, if right after you bought your home, someone comes out of the woodwork claiming that they still own the property from way back, and there is an investigation, and it's determined that they DO own the property due to some faulty recordkeeping 57 years ago, then title insurance will save your butt. Title insurance is NOT insurance on the home itself, or structural issues.
- There are fees associated with closing. These include title insurance fees, loan origination fees, etc. There may also be what we call "prepaids" which can include homeowners insurance, escrow payments for county property taxes, etc. There are too many options to cover them all here without boring you, but just make sure you ask your agent what all the fees will be so you aren't surprised. The one big one you should know about is homeowners insurance. You will need to get it before you can close, so you will need to meet with an insurance agent prior to the

date of closing. Homeowners insurance generally covers the following items: your dwelling, other structures on your property, personal property, and liability (for example in case someone is hurt on your property).

CLOSING IS COMPLICATED because so many stars have to align, but provided you have a good agent, and provided you don't do something foolhardy, it can be simple and even enjoyable. Having been in this business for quite some time, I've seen people make the same stupid mistakes over and over again at this point. Therefore, I have put together a helpful list to help you not screw up your closing.

Top 10 Stupid Ways to Screw up Closing

1. Incur new debt without telling your loan officer. Come on now, we talked about this! Don't get a new credit card, purchase a new car, buy $4,500 of new furniture for your new house (on your VISA card no less), without getting approval from your loan officer.
2. Forget to bring your down payment. Your loan officer will tell you how much money you need to bring to closing. It will be your down payment minus the earnest money you paid earlier (which is now being applied to your down payment). Bring this to closing! Don't blow it on a new home theatre system!
3. Forget that you had a bankruptcy or foreclosure. "Ah, Gee-dang-it! I forgot!" Yeah right...

Sometimes these things get missed on the credit report. But if you are dishonest (or just dumb) with your loan officer, and then the truth comes out at closing, you'll ruin the deal.

4. Quit your job. Don't quit your job, get fired, or suddenly decide to give up your career as a chemical engineer to pursue your *real* dream of being an alpaca farmer right before closing! That should be obvious, right?

5. Fail to bring documentation. Your realtor and loan officer should give you a list of documents to bring to closing. Things like proof of homeowners insurance, a VA certificate, ID cards, etc. These things are important! If you don't bring them, closing cannot happen. So put your big girl panties on, make yourself a list, and check it twice.

6. Get pissed during the final walkthrough. Maybe the seller trashed the place at the last second, or maybe the repairs just weren't done right. At this point, some people get pissed and walk away. Alternatively, you can just stand your ground and demand they fix it.

7. Change your mind. If you are one of those people prone to getting "buyer's remorse," try not to get it on the day of closing, okay? Ask yourself: do I freak out at the Walmart exit frequently, doubting whether I should have bought those jeans, that skirt, that 12 pack of Jillian Michaels workout dvds? Do I spend a lot of time at the customer service desk doing returns? If you answered yes to these questions, maybe you should take a Valium before coming to closing.*

Seriously though, chill out! It's a big decision, but it's not like you're buying a *house* or something...wait...

8. Fail to sell the home you are currently living in. Often, the success of your purchase is predicated upon the success of your sale; in other words, you have to sell your current house before you can buy your new one. If your sale falls through, so may your purchase. This one is not as much in your power to prevent. Still, do what you can, and be smart about keeping your realtor in the loop about everything that is going on with both deals.

9. Get a divorce. If there *is* a good time to get a divorce, this isn't it.

10. Uhhh...Okay, so I really only had *nine* dumb ways people commonly screw up closing, but a "top 9 list" just sounds retarded.

> * *I am not a doctor, and no sarcastic or metaphorical comments in this book should be construed as medical advice. Always consult a doctor before taking Diazepam (Valium) or any other heavy sedatives. Experience shows that you should also consult a doctor before starting a new Youtube exercise routine, juicing 2 pounds of kale, or undertaking a multi-day backpacking trek involving lamas.*

Step 9.5
After the Sale

AFTER THE SALE, there often occurs a common phenomena which I have come to refer to as "the ninety day rule." This rule states that in the ninety days after you buy your first house, something fairly significant will stop working, break, or otherwise go to pot. In my first house, the fridge went out. In our second house, the dishwasher and garage door stopped working. In our third house, the furnace *and* washing machine went kaput. I'm not sure why this happens, but it does. You can pretty much bank on it. *That,* by the way, is why home warranties are worth every penny.

AFTERWORD

There. It took some doing, but I've given you my brain. I hope you feel that way. I hope you feel empowered to buy a house. Remember what you learned here: <u>Get out of your own way</u> by getting real with yourself, knowing what you want, confronting reality, managing expectations, and overcoming common fears. <u>Work *with* your agent</u> by gaining enough knowledge to be dangerous yourself, and then having good communication skills. <u>Understand your power</u> as the buyer. Remember, you are a key decision maker and nothing rolls without you being on board. <u>Ask the right questions</u> by first, asking ALL of your questions, and second, being thoughtful and careful enough to ask some important questions that might not be obvious at first blush. <u>Dodge the landmines</u> by avoiding self-defeating behavior and common mistakes. <u>Don't be a jerk</u>; be respectful and courteous instead. Others will appreciate you for it, and your real estate experience will be so much the better. Understand the <u>Order of Operations</u>, and then follow them.

Now, my friend, go and do. Buy that house! Buy the crap out of it! You now know everything you need to.

...and, if you really loved this book, share it with all your friends. Or, if you don't have any friends (because you are living in your parent's basement as you read this), just go buy like 75 more copies of this book so that I can take my kids to Disneyland and buy myself that vintage WWII era beard comb I saw on eBay just now. Seriously, it's awesome...

Good luck!

11

BONUS

BONUS: Jack and Jill go up to Bill:
(An example real estate hunt and transaction)

NOW THAT YOU'VE read the book, I will present you with a mock real estate transaction to help you reflect and review what we have learned. The following may or may not be based on true events:

JACK AND JILL want to buy a house, so they go on Realtor.-com, find a property they like and click the infamous "we want more information" button.

> PRO TIP: *Don't click unless you want an agent*
> *to call you. Seems obvious right? Just know*
> *that there are at least 2 agents that could call,*
> *text or email you after you click.*

So, Being the savvy agent I am, I get in touch. Jack and Jill send me a list of homes they're interested in, to include the one they clicked on. We spend a few days looking at homes, and they find one they like. I go home, write up an offer, and submit it. The next day we get a counteroffer, but Jack and Jill decide that the terms are not favorable, so we continue to look around at other properties

.

NOTICE that the original trajectory and goals have shifted. It's a fluid thing, and this is where being guided by an agent can be particularly helpful. All the things mentioned in Hack #1 start off very clear, but often morph you start viewing real homes. This is okay! Just keep your agent in the loop on what direction you want to go. Keep in mind your agent will be trying their best to cater listings and showing to the best of their knowledge. If they don't *know* what you want, they can't *show* what you want (cheesy, but you get the point.)

JACK AND JILL'S focus has now shifted to newer townhomes. I set up a couple showings, and once again they want to put in an offer. I politely let Jack and Jill know that I'll be out of town the rest of the week, so I'll be sending them the offer electronically. They let me know that for various reasons, they are having someone else cosign with them.

A COUPLE THINGS TO note here: First, we have now written 2

offers. Second, Jill is Co-signing with Joni (Jills Mom) who used to be a realtor years ago. See how stuff gets complicated?

I GET a response the next day that the seller on the nicer newer townhome wants to counter. Jack, Jill, and Joni reject the counteroffer. Remember, I'm out of town; I have no control of what is going on back home. I *did* let Jack and Jill know that I have a team of agents that can help them while I was gone, if there is something I can't do from a distance. This is where working with your agent is a crucial step in this process.

> PRO TIP: *When you sign documents, make sure you read them thoroughly. As agents, we are to explain the contracts to the level of understanding of our clients. For some, that's "here are the docs please read and review." For others, it's "Let's go through this line by line together..." For others it's "Let me know if you have any questions." Make sure you and your agent both know how much help you require in this area. Communication and honesty are a key part in this process. When you are in "buying" mode, patience can be very hard to come by...*

JACK AND JILL decide they really want to buy, and become very frustrated that I left town. So, they contact "Bill," another realtor with a different company. For several weeks, Jack and Jill are looking at houses with Bill. Bill is not aware that Jack, Jill and Joni have signed a Buyer/Broker Agreement with me. Jack and Jill have gotten Bill to show them houses all over town and after a 2 or 3 weeks they decide to make an offer and they get one under contract.

IN SMALL TOWNS, news travels fast, and when things don't smell right, news travels even faster. So it is that I come to find out Jack and Jill are working with another agent. I tell myself I have a Buyer/Broker Agreement with these folks. I talk to Bill, and he had no knowledge of the alleged Buyer/Broker Agreement. So I reach out to Jack and Jill and learn that they are under contract on a house. He admits that while I was out of town they turned to another agent, and states that he was *very* helpful, and even sat down and explained things to them in person rather than emailing them. He says he's sorry for misleading me, but that Bill is just a better fit for them. Then he tells me to have a nice day.

I POLITELY EXPLAINED to Jack that, unfortunately, in the world of real estate, "have a nice rest of your day" is not how it works after you have signed legal documents, and tell him that lying to real estate agents is probably not the best way to go.

FORTUNATELY, nothing was done that couldn't be undone (apart from poor Bill getting cheated out of his time by Jack and Jill). They still got to buy the house, and they still had to pay me, since they had signed the agreement. But it left a bad taste in mouths all around.

. . .

THE GOOD NEWS IS, your real estate transactions don't have to be like that! If you follow the principals in this book, they can be painless! Enjoyable, even. Just remember, get a good agent, and *communicate* with them.

HAPPY HUNTING...